The Tale of Teeka

The Tale of Teeka

Michel Marc Bouchard

Translated by Linda Gaboriau

Talonbooks

1999

Copyright © 1999 Michel Marc Bouchard
Translation copyright © 1999 Linda Gaboriau

Published with the assistance of the Canada Council for the Arts.

We acknowledge the financial support of the Government of Canada through the Book Publishing Industry Development Program for our publishing activities. Canadä

Talonbooks
#104—3100 Production Way
Burnaby, British Columbia, Canada V5A 4R4

Typeset in Leawood and Garamond and printed and bound in Canada by Hignell Printing Ltd.

First Printing: February 1999

Talonbooks are distributed in Canada by General Distribution Services, 325 Humber College Blvd., Toronto, Ontario, Canada M9W 7C3; Tel.:(416) 213-1919; Fax:(416) 213-1917.
Talonbooks are distributed in the U.S.A. by General Distribution Services Inc., 85 Rock River Drive, Suite 202, Buffalo, New York, U.S.A. 14207-2170; Tel.:1-800-805-1083; Fax:1-800-481-6207.

L'Histoire de l'oie was published in the original French in 1991 by Leméac Éditeur, Montréal, Québec.

Canadian Cataloguing in Publication Data

Bouchard, Michel Marc, 1958-
  [Histoire de l'oie. English]
  The tale of Teeka

  A play.
  Translation of: L'histoire de l'oie.
  ISBN 0-88922-410-2

  I. Title. II. Title: Histoire de l'oie.
PS8553.O7745H5713 1999 C842'.54   C99-910226-5
PQ3919.2.B682H5713 1999

Contents

A Tale for Humiliated Children

1955. Rural Québec, caught between poverty and religious obscurantism. How were children raised in those days? With a stern eye and a firm grip, a wooden ruler and a leather strap! *The Tale of Teeka* is a story of laws.

A story about hereditary violence which, like poverty, is passed down from generation to generation.

My task was to find a way for Maurice to escape. The ways I found lead to the world of neurosis. Maurice prays to Bulamutumumo the way his parents pray to God. He longs to become Tarzan the way Teeka, the white goose, dreams of flying. He finds a partial but real solution by submitting to the beatings and by investing in the sordid barter these beatings obtain for him. These are his only means of escape.

He doesn't question the essence of this violence, it's all part of the laws.

Today there are still far more Maurices than we think. Boys and girls, men and women of all ages who remain as silent as ever.

I hope these humiliated children will read this text or see the show. I hope they will talk to someone about their misery. Talking about it ... Writing about it ... These are the first steps ... It doesn't eclipse the storm, but it calms the fury.

The Adventure

In 1986, Daniel Meilleur, artistic co-director of Théâtre des Deux Mondes, offered me the opportunity to write a play for young audiences. I embarked upon the adventure enthusiastically, accepting the challenge of writing a text which would reflect my inner world, without marginalizing the work on the pretext that it was for children's theatre. I was also anxious to offer this play to audiences of all ages.

Over a period of almost five years, with the assistance of Daniel Castonguay writing the visual images, Michel Robidoux writing the music, and Daniel Meilleur orchestrating the ensemble, I periodically plunged myself into the world of Maurice and Teeka, and of Edgar Rice Burroughs' *Tarzan*. My artistic objectives became clearer: I wanted to write the most minimalist of all my plays; fewer words and more emphasis on the power of evocation.

It was a memorable adventure. From the magnificent creative retreats in Cap-à-l'Aigle and Pointe-Fortune to the theatre-lab space at Théâtre des Deux Mondes, we re-examined theatre for young audiences, reinvented the world ... and savoured the pleasure of working together.

I had the good fortune, at four different stages, of hearing my text presented in semi-public performances for audiences which included, among others, the Théâtre des Deux Mondes advisory committee.

I want to express my thanks to Louis Roy, Vincent Gratton, Normand Bissonnette, Alain Fournier and Yves Dagenais, the actors who participated in the creative process, and to the artists and craftsmen who worked on Daniel Castonguay's superb set. And last but not least, I want to pay tribute to Théâtre des Deux Mondes and their commitment to developing new work.

—Michel Marc Bouchard

The Tale of Teeka

L'Histoire de l'oie was first produced in June 1991, at the annual *Rencontres internationales Théâtre et jeunes spectateurs* in Lyon, France, by Théâtre des Deux Mondes (Montreal), in collaboration with the National Arts Centre's Théâtre Français (Ottawa). The production was directed by Daniel Meilleur, designed by Daniel Castonguay, with music composed by Michel Robidoux. It was first presented in Canada in November 1991, at Montreal's Théâtre d'Aujourd'hui, under the artistic direction of Michelle Rossignol with the following cast:

MAURICE (CHILD)	Yves Dagenais
MAURICE (ADULT)	Alain Fournier

The English translation, *The Tale of Teeka*, was first produced by Théâtre des Deux Mondes, with the original cast, at the World Stage Festival in Toronto in June 1992.

Since the world premiere in 1991, Théâtre des Deux Mondes and the original cast have presented and continue to present, their widely acclaimed production in French, English, German and

Spanish, representing Canada at numerous international festivals and garnering rave reviews and several prizes in Dublin, Glasgow, Hong Kong, Limoges, London, Mexico City, Munich, and at the Brooklyn Academy of Music in New York.

Most recently, the play has been successfully produced by companies in Germany and Belgium. Adapted for television by the playwright, translated by Linda Gaboriau and directed by Tim Southam, *The Tale of Teeka* will be seen on the CBC national network in April 1999.

Characters

MAURICE (ADULT): A man in his early thirties. He will manipulate the puppet for TEEKA, the white goose.

MAURICE (CHILD): A boy of nine.

Setting

Late summer, 1955. A farm house with its outbuildings, enclosed by a fence. An overall impression of austerity. A storm is brewing in the distance.

The Tale of Teeka

MAURICE (ADULT)
> There are stories we are told only when we're
> young, there are others we are told as
> adults … Most of the stories we are told as
> adults should be told to us when we are
> children … The story I'm going to tell you is
> the kind of story I should have been told when
> I was young.

> It was the end of a very hot day.

> *MAURICE (CHILD) enters carrying two pails; one
> is empty, the other contains goose droppings. He
> fills the empty pail with water. The need to
> urinate makes him shiver. We suddenly hear the
> muffled rumble of a storm in the distance.*

MAURICE (ADULT)
> A storm was gathering in the distance. It
> hovered over three quarters of the horizon.

> *MAURICE (CHILD) drops his chores and climbs
> onto the roof of the house.*

MAURICE (ADULT)

Maurice sat down at the centre of the universe.

MAURICE (CHILD)

(*sombre and threatening*) I want the wind to bring you here.

MAURICE (ADULT)

That voice was the voice he used when he set ants on fire in a cardboard box, the voice he used when he tore the wings off butterflies.

MAURICE (CHILD)

I want you to come closer!

MAURICE (ADULT)

The sky grew dark and menacing.

MAURICE (CHILD)

I want you to come here.

MAURICE (ADULT)

The wind raised little tornadoes of dry straw.

MAURICE (CHILD)

Make me feel scared!

MAURICE (ADULT)

The leaves in the trees trembled ever so
slightly.

MAURICE (CHILD)

That's right. Make me feel scared!

MAURICE (ADULT)

Rusty with age, the chains on the swings
began to complain. The doors of the barn
banged together, as if someone or something
was trying to escape.

MAURICE (CHILD)

(*raising his arms toward the sky*) Come here!

MAURICE (ADULT)

Heaven and earth had the same density. Wary
of the storm about to strike, groundhogs,
toads, sparrows grew still. The wind ceased.
All nature fell silent.

MAURICE (CHILD)

(*gently*) BULAMUTUMUMO!

MAURICE (ADULT)

The first rumblings were heard answering
Maurice's call!

MAURICE (CHILD)

BULAMUTUMUMO!

MAURICE (ADULT)

He was calling the great God of the jungle, the
one not even Tarzan would have dared disturb.

MAURICE (CHILD)

BULAMUTUMUMO! I want you to strike
our house.

MAURICE (ADULT)

Closer this time, the heavy voice answered
again. (*rumbling*)

MAURICE (CHILD)

I want to see it explode into a thousand pieces!

MAURICE (ADULT)

In the distance, the sound of rain joined the
deafening procession of approaching thunder.

MAURICE (CHILD)

BULAMUTUMUMO! Now! Strike now!
Obey me! Here, on my house!

One, two, three ... (*thunder*)

MAURICE (ADULT)

The wind began to blow with extraordinary
rage. The swings waltzed faster and faster. The
smell of wet earth filled the air.

MAURICE (CHILD)

Destroy it! (*thunder*)

MAURICE (ADULT)

Huge drops of rain began to fall on his head.

MAURICE (CHILD)

Set it on fire!

MAURICE (ADULT)

The uproar prevented him from hearing a
voice calling from inside the house, begging
him to come in and take shelter. "Get down
from there! Maurice! Get down!"

MAURICE (CHILD)
    Here, on our house!

MAURICE (ADULT)
    Get in the house!

MAURICE (CHILD)
    One, two, three … (*thunder*) Closer! Louder!

MAURICE (ADULT)
    Maurice! Get in the house!

MAURICE (CHILD)
    Louder!

MAURICE (ADULT)
    Lightning struck not far from the house.
    Maurice felt that he had been obeyed.
    Suddenly, he heard the voice begging him to
    come down from the roof. Frightened, he
    obeyed that voice. (*MAURICE (CHILD) climbs
    down from the roof and disappears behind the
    house.*) Only then did lightning strike, several
    times, on his head, his body and most of all
    his arms! For a fraction of a second, Maurice
    thought it was the thunderstorm … (*beat*) It
    was not the thunderstorm. The anger of

Bulamutumumo was fading in the distance. The sound of groundhogs, toads and sparrows could be heard once again.

Enter TEEKA, a white goose puppet manipulated and played by MAURICE (ADULT).

TEEKA

I loved thunderstorms. The sky released showers of earthworms, plump and ready to eat. And this time, they were all for me. It was one of the few advantages I found in my solitude.

I lived in a very small house near Maurice's. Earlier that week, my house had suddenly become too big for me. I had watched all my fellow-geese enter the barn ... and I never saw them come out again.

(*observing the earthworms*) This one or that one? I'll turn the first one to move into a mere mouthful! He moved! Let's allow him to wriggle a bit longer, enjoy the few seconds he has left. A bit of play, in the name of sportsmanship! On your mark, gulp! (*She eats it.*)

My own mother had disappeared into the barn when I was only a gosling. That was the day I met Maurice. He brought me a handful of insects, dead and mutilated. I was touched by his gesture but I tried to explain that this was not my usual fare. (*She honks.*) My voice frightened him. He dropped the poor butterflies that he had transformed back into caterpillars and fled.

Another one moved! He obviously has no sense of danger! Innocent creature! Too much pity leads to famine. Gulp!

She eats the worm.

The following day, I decided to adopt a more tameable attitude. This time, Maurice offered me some grain ... I allowed myself to be tempted ... It wasn't the delectable grain my fellow-geese had ingurgitated several days before disappearing into the barn, but it was tastier than what they usually made me eat. (*She honks.*) My voice frightened him again.

I realize the song of the white goose is much less melodious than that of the swallow or even the chirping of sparrows which I personally find unbearable.

Yet in some countries we replace watchdogs and we honk at the slightest sign of danger. Remember the Geese on Capitoline Hill! Yes, it was my ancestors who alerted the sleeping Romans upon the arrival of the invader. We are very proud of this historical exploit and the story is transmitted from gander to egg.

Another one who dared move! Unfortunately for them, earthworms don't honk! Such a pity!! Gulp! (*She eats the earthworm.*)

Maurice came back for the third day in a row. It was his turn to frighten me. As I was allowing him to pat my neck, he began to tear out some feathers. I am not an ant, nor a butterfly … I bit him …

That is how we tamed our solitudes. (*to the earthworms*) Their sluggishness exasperates me! Gulp!

My long days were filled with the memory of my fellow-geese and our conversations about tomorrow's weather, about different grooming techniques and stories of our glorious past. But I had discovered another pastime: observing Maurice.

MAURICE (CHILD) finally comes out of the house. His arm is in a sling.

MAURICE (CHILD)
(*In the doorway, as if talking to someone.*) Yes! Yes! Yes!

The door closes.

TEEKA
What had happened to his arm?

MAURICE (CHILD)
It's nothing serious, Teeka. My arm is taking a nap.

TEEKA
I was relieved. His arm was resting.

MAURICE (CHILD)

(*unenthusiastically*) He gave me his brand new cap!

TEEKA

His glasses were miraculously clean.

MAURICE (CHILD)

He said they were going to get me a real Tarzan costume. Soon.

TEEKA

He had wanted one for ages.

MAURICE (CHILD)

Teeka, look what I have for you! (*He shows her a piece of cake.*)

TEEKA

I didn't know whether I should approach him ... He often spoiled me, but cake ...

MAURICE (CHILD)

It's new cake.

TEEKA

    I knew it would cost me a few feathers ... but
    for cake ...

MAURICE (CHILD)

    I didn't even have to steal it ...

TEEKA

    But for cake ...

MAURICE (CHILD)

    She gave it to me for you. She knew it would
    make me happy.

TEEKA

    But for cake, I was willing to be plucked bare.

    She goes over to him. She eats some cake.

MAURICE (CHILD)

    Eat, Teeka!

TEEKA

It was one of the most beautiful moments in my life. There were earthworms lying on the ground everywhere, I was eating new cake and Maurice was patting my neck without pulling out a single feather.

MAURICE (CHILD)

(*singing unenthusiastically*) "Oh happy times. We're all just fine. Oh happy times."

MAURICE (CHILD)

(*patting her*) Eat, Teeka!

TEEKA

Teeka! I loved that name. All the more because in the eyes of the other geese, I had a personality. Teeka! They were a bit jealous.

MAURICE (CHILD)

(*looking toward the house and mumbling*) Today it struck pretty close …

TEEKA

Especially since they couldn't say my name properly. Pronouncing the "tee" in Teeka was a veritable feat of diction.

MAURICE (CHILD)
> Like the ants ...

TEEKA
> Since it was my name, I had managed to
> overcome the difficulty ...

MAURICE (CHILD)
> Like the butterflies ...

TEEKA
> ... my honour was at stake. (*shouting*) "Teeka!"

MAURICE (CHILD)
> Not so loud!

TEEKA
> (softly) Teeka!

MAURICE (CHILD)
> Eat. I have chores to do.

*He goes to fill the pail with water and it makes
him want to urinate. TEEKA doesn't eat. She goes
over to MAURICE (CHILD) and prevents him from
working.*

MAURICE (CHILD)

I don't have time. I have to finish my chores.
Go eat your cake. Stop! You're going to get a
kick! (*TEEKA manages to take the comic book out
of the back pocket of MAURICE's pants.*) Teeka!
Give that back to me! Give it to me, I don't
have time to read! (*She shakes her head yes.*)
Later! (*She shakes her head no.*) Alright, just
one page! (*She shakes her head yes, several
times.*)

*TEEKA gives him his comic book and goes to eat
her cake. MAURICE (CHILD) wants to hold her.
She pulls away. She comes back gently. He pats
her.*

MAURICE (CHILD)

(*reading*) Tarzan was still an infant when, in a
terrible outburst of rage, Bulamutumumo
shattered the ship carrying Lord and Lady
Greystoke ... (*He stops reading.*) ... his mum
and his dad.

TEEKA

He looked at his house the way my
fellow-geese used to look at the barn.

MAURICE (CHILD)

That's enough. I have work to do.

TEEKA starts honking loudly.

MAURICE (CHILD)

Stop! Don't make them come out of the house!
Stop!

She continues to honk.

MAURICE (CHILD)

I have to go clean up the barn.

TEEKA

I wanted to follow him but ...

MAURICE (CHILD)

No, you can't come in the barn!

She honks.

MAURICE (CHILD)

I'll tell you a secret. Then you have to let me
work ... (*Silence.*)

Teeka? (*Unenthusiastically, she nods her agreement.*)

Today I read in a book that the white goose stood for the number 5 in Ancient Egypt. 1, 2, 3, 4, goose. I have "goose" fingers on each hand. (*He laughs.*) In another book, I learned that the angels copied their wings from yours.

TEEKA

I was bursting with pride ... and the cake got stuck in my crop.

MAURICE (CHILD)

Now, you're going to be an angel and let me do my chores.

TEEKA

No. I wanted him to stay!

TEEKA prevents him from working. She finally makes MAURICE (CHILD) trip and spill the pails all over himself.

MAURICE (CHILD)

Why did you do that?

TEEKA

I had dirtied his clothes.

MAURICE (CHILD)

(*angry*) You got no brains!

TEEKA

Young humans, not having feathers, don't
clean what they wear themselves. Their parents
buy, sew and clean everything that covers their
offspring's skin.

MAURICE (CHILD)

They're going to say I did it on purpose again!
Come over here!

TEEKA

I turned even whiter! (*She goes towards him
cautiously.*)

*We hear the door to the house close. Then the
sound of the doors on the farm truck slamming
shut and the engine starting up.*

MAURICE (CHILD)

(*hiding*) Yes! … Yes! …

TEEKA

> I would have loved to see him act courageous, like when he faced the storm and challenged Bulamutumumo ... Streaks of mud were pouring down his cheeks. I couldn't tell whether they were tears. I saw the farm truck go rattling through the puddles. The roar of the engine faded in the distance. For the second time that day, nature fell silent. I was saved.

MAURICE (CHILD)

> Come over here!

TEEKA

> No, thank you!

> *Once TEEKA is close enough, MAURICE lowers his arm into the puddle and splashes her. She begins to stomp in the water and splashes him back. They stop, breathless.*

MAURICE (CHILD)

> So there, I did that on purpose! (*He smears mud over his face.*) And I did that on purpose, too! (*Beat.*) They'll be back in two hours. They've gone to the market to sell ... to sell ...

TEEKA

He didn't finish his sentence.

MAURICE (CHILD)

(*worried*) Your feathers are too soft ...

TEEKA

For the very first time, we were the only ones
in the world!

MAURICE (CHILD)

Come on, we have time to wash before they
get back ... Come on, Teeka, I'll introduce you
to Tarzan ... We'll go for a swim in the sea!

He heads toward the house.

TEEKA

The prospect of entering that house didn't
really appeal to me. Maurice wanted so badly
to see Bulamutumumo destroy it ... It seemed
so frightening ... He opened the screen door
and we entered Tarzan's home: the jungle.

MAURICE (CHILD)

Be careful, there are poisonous snakes,
quicksand, deadly insects ...

TEEKA

Frankly, this wasn't very reassuring ... There
were indeed some strange things ... Here
and there, little balls of fire were trapped in
glass ... They provided the light in the house
... On the wall, there were humans in frames,
their heads always staring in the same
direction without moving ... The snakes
must have paralyzed them like this with their
venom ... There was another one nailed to
pieces of wood in the shape of a cross ... And
on either side of him also in frames, a human
male and a female whose hearts were
exposed ... a whole family killed by insects, I
assumed ... (*A pair of boots is drying in the
staircase, upside down.*) That human must have
been dragged under by the quicksand ...

MAURICE (CHILD)

The swamps exhale fatal smells.

TEEKA

The house did exhale a fatal smell ... of freshly
baked cake. Certainly it was a trap! And not a
trace of Tarzan ... Suddenly I heard bells ...
(*She honks.*) A bird popped out of his wooden
cage and called at least seven times ... before

disappearing. (*Cuckoo! Cuckoo!*) Undoubtedly a cry of distress ... I wanted to rescue him, but then I realized that Maurice had disappeared too. Had he been dragged under by the slippery floor where I had left the prints of my webbed feet? (*We hear the sound of running water.*) That had to be the famous waterfall near the river, the river that seemed so important to Maurice ... Tarzan.

MAURICE (CHILD)
(*voice off*) I'm in the sea, Teeka.

TEEKA
Well! He had already found the sea. It seemed a pity to rush the story like that. "You'll have to excuse me, Cuckoo, but they're waiting to introduce me to Tarzan. I'll be back to save you soon!"

She joins MAURICE (CHILD) in the bathroom. He has taken off his clothes.

MAURICE (CHILD)
Come jump in the sea.

TEEKA

Maurice had often spoken of the sea. But this
was the first time I had ever seen it. It was all
white, and so small. (*She approaches the
bathtub. She notices the many bruises on
MAURICE's body.*) Why was Bulamutumumo
so hard on Maurice's body? Why didn't his
arm wake up?

MAURICE (CHILD)

(*Embarrassed to see TEEKA looking at him.*) It's
nothing serious, Teeka. It's just because ...
because ...

TEEKA

Once again, he did not finish his sentence.

MAURICE (CHILD)

They're just injuries I got in the jungle
fighting with Numa, the lion ... Come for a
swim ...

TEEKA

(*jumping into the tub*) Gracefully, I floated the
way my elders had once told me we were able.

MAURICE (CHILD)
> I also learned, in another book, that you are
> the symbol of "fidelity." That means we are
> always going to think about each other.

TEEKA
> If he stopped tearing out my feathers and
> brought me new cake every day, I would
> happily pledge my fidelity to him.

MAURICE (CHILD)
> (*Singing more enthusiastically while washing
> his clothes.*)
> "Oh, happy times. We're all just fine. Oh,
> happy times."
>
> *MAURICE (CHILD) takes the bar of soap.*

MAURICE (CHILD)
> This is a bar of soap. It's a precious stone the
> great witch doctors from the Gomangani tribe
> invented so they could be clean.
>
> *He shows TEEKA how to use soap.*

TEEKA

Couldn't the witch doctors' precious stone, this "soap," make his injuries disappear?

MAURICE (CHILD)

I already told you. It's the lion.

TEEKA

Was there another story to be told?

MAURICE (CHILD)

Listen, Teeka! This is the first time I've ever brought a friend here. I don't want anything to go wrong.

MAURICE (CHILD) wraps a towel around his waist and climbs out of the tub.

TEEKA

Dressed like that, Maurice had all the splendour of Tarzan, king of the jungle.

MAURICE goes up to TEEKA's face, affectionately.

MAURICE (CHILD)

I am Tarzan. Tarzan will protect you. Because Tarzan is all powerful. The best of everything in the jungle will be yours.

TEEKA

It was an oath of fidelity.

MAURICE (CHILD)

I need a weapon ...

MAURICE (CHILD) discovers a leather strap. He hits his hand with it twice.

MAURICE (CHILD)

This vine will protect us. It is powerful. And dangerous ... It will protect us.

TEEKA

Nearby, there was another sea, a tiny one.

TEEKA jumps into the toilet. MAURICE (CHILD) pulls the chain.

TEEKA

I heard Numa the lion roar and I felt myself
being pulled down as if Bulamutumumo
wanted to devour me. (*She honks.*)

MAURICE grabs her and pulls her out of the toilet.
With his intact arm, he awkwardly beats his
chest and lets out Tarzan's traditional call.

TEEKA

There was no doubt about it. It was Tarzan
standing there before me.

MAURICE (CHILD)

Let's go, Teeka!

TEEKA

A unique adventure was in store for me. A
pity I wouldn't be able to relate it to my
fellow-geese.

They head towards the bedroom. We hear the
cuckoo call once.

TEEKA

I'll be right there, Cuckoo! And there we were,
heading into the bush. The jungle was full of
doors. Here and there, trees had been planted
in pots. There were more of those human
heads captured in frames staring at me. We
crossed the smooth, shiny ground of a vast
clearing where there was food in great
abundance. And off to one side, a white basin
with water. A sea much more agitated than the
others. It washed back and forth, making
bubbles. Suddenly I saw the arm of a piece of
human clothing emerge, then sink again.
Another call for help? I looked around me ...
Cakes! Not one, not two, not three, goose
cakes sat regally on the windowsill. I thought I
was dreaming. I wanted to go closer ...

(*The phone rings.*) I ran to take shelter. I
examined the animal that had emitted this
sound. A jet black animal that was clinging to
the wall. Maurice ... Tarzan grabbed it by the
ears ...

MAURICE (CHILD)

Hello? Yes. No, not yet. I'll do it right away.
Yes. Yes. Bye. (*He hangs up.*)

TEEKA

To my great relief, Tarzan had tamed the beast.

MAURICE (CHILD)

Let's continue on our way, Teeka!

TEEKA

(*Speaking of MAURICE's bedroom.*)
He opened a door and we plunged into the
unknown. There was a small enclosure in this
room. It was fenced in at both ends with
wooden bars, but the longer sides had no
barriers. There was also an opening covered
with glass where Kudu the Sun could enter.

MAURICE (CHILD)

This is my bed, Teeka!

TEEKA

So that was what they called "a bed?" Maurice
had often told me how much he hated going
"to bed" without my understanding what he
meant. So this was Maurice's pen?

*MAURICE (CHILD) picks up TEEKA and settles her
on the bed.*

MAURICE (CHILD)

You take the pillow, Teeka. You'll be more
comfortable.

TEEKA

"Pillow." What a strange word for that fluffy
bag.

*MAURICE (CHILD) introduces his collection of
miniature animals.*

MAURICE (CHILD)

This is Numa, the lion. Dingo, the hyena ...
Sheeta, the panther ... Manu, the monkey
with the long tail ... Bara, the deer ... Sabor,
the lioness ... And Tantor, the elephant.

TEEKA

It was an important moment. I was
surrounded by all of Tarzan's friends.

*MAURICE (CHILD) takes a small box out from
under his bed.*

TEEKA

A cookie box! I was going to eat again!

*MAURICE (CHILD) takes his Tarzan comic book
out of the box.*

TEEKA
  It wasn't cookies!

MAURICE (CHILD)
  (*reading the title*) "Tarzan's Nightmare."

TEEKA
  Why a nightmare? Why not a happy dream?

MAURICE (CHILD)
  A nightmare is when they turn out all the
  lights. And a dream is when they leave one
  light on. "Tarzan's Nightmare."

*He opens the book and the animals come to life.
The leaves and the trees printed on the bedspread
rise and begin to sway in the wind that enters
through the window. Vines fall from the ceiling
… The walls of the room fade and are replaced
by mountains and valleys and cliffs.*

MAURICE (CHILD)
  One day Tarzan was very hungry.

TEEKA

Just like me!

MAURICE (CHILD)

He saw an old man from the Gomangani tribe eating the flesh of Tantor, the elephant.

TEEKA

An elephant! I would have been satisfied with a cookie.

MAURICE (CHILD)

Shhhh! When night fell and the old man had eaten his fill, Tarzan took advantage of his drowsiness and stole a piece of the elephant meat.

Tantor lets out a final sigh and plays dead. MAURICE (CHILD) picks up Tantor and pretends to eat him.

MAURICE (CHILD)

"Now, his stomach heavy, it was Tarzan's turn to doze. Suddenly, he heard a cry! (*Numa, the miniature lion, roars.*) What, morning already?

Is it possible that I've already slept? Then he saw the lion crouched beside him, about to pounce."

TEEKA

I noticed that the lion and his female, Sabor, had come dangerously close to Maurice. I could see the saliva flowing from their drooping jowls and their canine teeth preparing to seize him.

MAURICE (CHILD)

"Tarzan climbed the tree. He turned to make a face at the lion, expecting to see him at the foot of the tree, but much to his astonishment, Numa had followed. Tarzan kept climbing higher until he reached the supple branches of the tree. The lion was still at his heels. It was unimaginable."

TEEKA

Dingo, the hyena, sneered and laughed as he watched the scene, anticipating the leftovers from the feast.

MAURICE (CHILD)

I'm caught in the trap!

TEEKA

Sheeta, the panther, prepared for the battle
over Tarzan's corpse.

MAURICE (CHILD)

I can't climb any higher!

TEEKA

Bara, the deer, and Manu, the monkey with
the long tail, had taken refuge and were
trembling with fear under the tallest tree.

MAURICE (CHILD)

Save me, Teeka!

TEEKA

Tarzan was moving farther and farther away
from me. An immense valley lay between us.

MAURICE (CHILD)

Help, Teeka, help!

TEEKA

I can't!

MAURICE (CHILD)

Yes, you can!

TEEKA

I had to save him. I had no choice. I beat
my wings as hard as I could ... harder ... and
harder!

MAURICE (CHILD)

Harder!

TEEKA

And like an angel I rose into the air. I flew to
Tarzan's rescue. I was graceful, majestic.

MAURICE (CHILD)

Hurry, Teeka! The lion is about to sink his
long teeth into my arm!

TEEKA

I dove down to rescue him.

MAURICE (CHILD)

Look at your feet, Teeka. You're growing talons
as sharp as knives.

TEEKA

Terrified, I stared at the long hooks that were
growing at the end of my webbed feet.

MAURICE (CHILD)
Sink them into my skin, dig them into my flesh and carry me away!

TEEKA
I was horrified. (*Beat.*)

MAURICE (CHILD)
Obey me!

TEEKA
(*confused*) I was so happy to play with Tarzan, to discover his jungle, I was happy to fly ...

MAURICE (CHILD)
Will you listen to me when I speak to you?

TEEKA
Was I to pay for this happiness by torturing him?

MAURICE (CHILD)
I'm going to take out the strap! Sink your hooks into my back!

TEEKA
I couldn't bring myself to do it.

MAURICE (CHILD)

You know what you're going to get if you don't
do as I say!

TEEKA

He was torturing me, as if it were vital that I
wound him!

MAURICE (CHILD)

The lion is going to devour me, Teeka! You
want to make me feel bad, is that it?

TEEKA

I longed to stop flying but there seemed to be
no end to the labyrinth of this nightmare. It
was as if someone else was talking through
him ...

MAURICE (CHILD)

I said "now!"

TEEKA

The more he yelled at me, the longer my
talons grew!

MAURICE (CHILD)

Right now!

TEEKA
No!

MAURICE (CHILD)
I'll never play with you again! Never, ever
again!

*He beats the pillow with the leather strap so hard
a cloud of feathers rises into the air.*

TEEKA
We both stood still, appalled ... in the midst of
a shower of feathers ...

*The animals climb back into the cookie box.
Once again, the leaves become a design on the
bedspread, and the valleys, mountains and cliffs
fade away. Kudu the Sun allows Goro the Moon
to take his place.*

MAURICE (CHILD)
(*rushing over to* TEEKA *and holding her tight*)
"... and the bird carried Tarzan to the edge of
the sea. He was safe at last. And then he woke
with a start. It was a bad dream ... a bad
dream."

TEEKA

The pillow was stuffed with goose feathers. It was the feathers of my fellow-geese that were floating all around us. This pillow was the ultimate destination, from the pen to the barn. And perhaps my only friend slept every night, with his head resting on my mother's down. (*She pulls away.*) No! I didn't want him to hold me in his arms. He had broken our oath of fidelity.

MAURICE (CHILD)

(*upset*) That's how it is, Teeka. That's the way things are and there's nothing we can do about it. Nothing!

TEEKA lets out a long cry and leaves the room.

MAURICE (CHILD)

Stay here! I'll give you some cake!

MAURICE (CHILD) leaves the room.

TEEKA

Maurice had known all along. Maurice knew exactly what was awaiting me. Maurice knew, yet did nothing to save me from this cruel fate.

MAURICE (CHILD)

    I'll tell you a story. A beautiful story!

TEEKA

    Out! I wanted to get out of there! I slid across
the smooth, shiny floor. I was no longer the
majestic goose flying to Tarzan's rescue. I was
an awkward prey, stumbling with every step,
looking more and more ridiculous. The more
I panicked, the more lost I felt in the maze of
Maurice's jungle. I tried to retrace my
footsteps, but kept going round in circles.

MAURICE (CHILD)

    Come here!

TEEKA

    He was trying to tempt me. All of a sudden, I
found myself standing face to face with
another goose. I felt relieved. "Tell me the way
out." She was making the same gesture I was.
"Tell me the way out." The nightmare
continued. "Tell me the way out." I wanted to
follow her, but her image shattered into a
thousand pieces.

We hear the sound of a mirror shattering.

MAURICE (CHILD)
Stop, Teeka. You're going to break everything.

TEEKA
I flapped my wings and found myself at the peak of the jungle. Maurice had followed me.

In the attic, near a window.

MAURICE (CHILD)
Come here!

TEEKA
I didn't dare look at him. Inside the only frame in that room, I saw two bright, shining eyes ... Eyes that were becoming more and more dazzling ... growing larger and larger ... Maurice was the first to understand ...

MAURICE (CHILD)
It's the headlights on the truck. They're home. They said two hours. It hasn't been two hours.

TEEKA

He didn't know whether he should run to the bathroom and gather up his wet clothes, or hurry to sweep the pieces of broken mirror, or get rid of the feathers that had filled his room.

MAURICE (CHILD) stands stock still, frozen in terror. The hum of the engine becomes louder and louder.

MAURICE (CHILD)

(*horrified*) If they find you in the house, I'm dead!

Long silence.

TEEKA

That day, the nocturnal birds did not follow the diurnal birds. As nature fell silent for the third time, I understood what Maurice's life was like in that jungle. I dared look at him, knowing it was my only hope … That look held all the tenderness distress can convey! Let's escape together! Escape far from your house, far from the barn, far from the jungle! Far, far away!

MAURICE (CHILD)

    I can't help it, Teeka. That's the way things are.

He grabs the goose's neck and breaks it.

MAURICE (CHILD)

    Afterwards ... after ... If they've really hurt
me ... I'll get my Tarzan costume.

MAURICE (ADULT)

    Just as Teeka felt her bones snap, she spread
her wings and flew for the second time that
day. She flew so high she disappeared beyond
the clouds. I was her only friend ... I was her
executioner. Once again, the sky grew dark.
Once again, the storm struck at the heart of
the house. The wind raised small tornadoes of
feathers from the pillow, he swept up the
pieces of mirror, and erased Teeka's wet
footprints. (*Thunder and lightning rage in the
heart of the house.*)

MAURICE (ADULT)

    The storm still rages at the centre of my being.
I hope some day this fury will give way to
calm.

MAURICE (CHILD) appears on the roof of the house, dressed in his brand new Tarzan costume, a bandage around his head.

MAURICE (CHILD)
Bulamutumumo! Bulamutumumo! Bulamutumumo!

CHORUS OF CHILDREN
(voice off) Oh, happy times. We're all just fine. Oh, happy times!

THE END